HIP-HOP

Usher

Raymond Lord

Mason Crest Publishers

Usher

FRONTIS The "Godson of Soul," Usher has won fans worldwide for his music, acting, charitable works, and good looks.

PRODUCED BY 21ST CENTURY PUBLISHING AND COMMUNICATIONS, INC.

EDITORIAL BY HARDING HOUSE PUBLISHING SERVICES, INC.

MASON CREST PUBLISHERS INC.
370 Reed Road
Broomall, Pennsylvania 19008
(866)MCP-BOOK (toll free)
www.masoncrest.com

Printed in Malaysia.

First Printing

9 8 7 6 5 4 3 2 1

Library of Congress Cataloging-in-Publication Data

Lord, Raymond.
    Usher / by Raymond Lord.
        p. cm. — (Hip-hop)
    Includes index.
ISBN 1-4222-0131-7
    1. Usher—Juvenile literature. 2. Rhythm and blues musicians—United States—Biography—Juvenile literature. I. Title. II. Series.
ML3930.U84L67 2007
782.421643092—dc22
                                                              2006005692

Publisher's notes:
- All quotations in this book come from original sources, and contain the spelling and grammatical inconsistencies of the original text.

- The Web sites mentioned in this book were active at the time of publication. The publisher is not responsible for Web sites that have changed their addresses or discontinued operation since the date of publication. The publisher will review and update the Web site addresses each time the book is reprinted.

Contents

Hip-Hop Timeline

1974 Hip-hop pioneer Afrika Bambaataa organizes the Universal Zulu Nation.

1988 *Yo! MTV Raps* premieres on MTV.

1970s Hip-hop as a cultural movement begins in the Bronx, New York City.

1985 *Krush Groove*, a hip-hop film about Def Jam Recordings, is released featuring Run-D.M.C., Kurtis Blow, LL Cool J, and the Beastie Boys.

1970s DJ Kool Herc pioneers the use of breaks, isolations, and repeats using two turntables.

1979 The Sugarhill Gang's song "Rapper's Delight" is the first hip-hop single to go gold.

1986 Run-D.M.C. are the first rappers to appear on the cover of *Rolling Stone* magazine.

1970   1980   1988

1976 Grandmaster Flash & the Furious Five pioneer hip-hop MCing and freestyle battles.

1986 Beastie Boys' album *Licensed to Ill* is released and becomes the best-selling rap album of the 1980s.

1970s Break dancing emerges at parties and in public places in New York City.

1982 Afrika Bambaataa embarks on the first European hip-hop tour.

1988 Hip-hop music annual record sales reaches $100 million.

1970s Graffiti artist Vic pioneers tagging on subway trains in New York City.

1984 *Graffiti Rock*, the first hip-hop television program, premieres.

1993 Rapper Snoop Dogg's album *Doggystyle* is the first debut album to hit the music charts at number one.

2006 Queen Latifah becomes the first hip-hop artist to receive a star on the Hollywood Walk of Fame.

1989 DJ Jazzy Jeff & The Fresh Prince become the first hip-hop artists to win a Grammy Award.

2003 Rapper Eminem becomes the first hip-hop artist to win an Academy Award.

2005 Hip-hop artist Kanye West appears on the cover of *Time* magazine.

1989 Rap is added as a new category to the *Billboard* charts.

1997 East Coast rapper Notorious B.I.G. (aka Biggie Smalls) is murdered.

2004 First National Hip-Hop Political Convention is held in Newark, New Jersey.

1989   2000   2006

1990s Hip-hop emerges in Europe.

1996 West Coast rapper Tupac Shakur is shot and killed.

2005 Rapper Will Smith opens the Philadelphia Live 8 concert as part of 10 simultaneous concerts held worldwide to bring attention to the extreme poverty in Africa.

1989 First gangsta rap album, *Straight Outta Compton*, is released by N.W.A.

2001 The hip-hop political action group, Hip-Hop Summit Action Network, is founded by Russell Simmons.

1992 Dr. Dre's album *The Chronic* is released; it redefines West Coast rap.

2006 The Smithsonian Institute National Museum of American History announces the creation of a new hip-hop exhibition scheduled to open in three to five years.

Usher won a phenomenal eleven awards at the 2004 Billboard Music Awards. He also won awards that year from MTV, World Music Awards, Radio Music Awards, Source Hip-Hop Music Awards, American Music Awards, and even the Nordic Music Awards.

1

Award Winner

Every year, *Billboard* gives awards to the year's most talented musicians. In 2004, eleven of those awards went to a single artist, a man who seemed too young to have achieved such success. With his smooth, sexy looks, *Rolling Stone* had called him an "**R&B** teen dream." But his awards proved he was all grown up now.

His name was Usher.
He explained on his official Web site, usherworld.com:

❝I have been building my career since I was a little boy, because singing had always been what I wanted to do. At first I thought about playing [professional] football, then I wanted to play basketball, but in the end it was all about the music. It's my biggest passion and my biggest joy.❞

On that night in 2004, Usher must have felt as though all his dreams had come true. With all his life's ups and downs, he had come a long way in a very short time.

Childhood

On October 14, 1978, in Dallas, Texas, a son was born to Usher Raymond III and Jonetta Patton. They named him Usher Raymond IV, honoring the long heritage of pride that went before him. They probably never suspected, though, how famous he would make the name of Usher!

When Usher was a year old, his parents divorced, and Usher moved with his mother, who is known as J-Pat, to Chattanooga, Tennessee. There, J-Pat remarried, and Usher's little brother, James, was born. Usher and James grew up close in more than just years.

Usher's musical talents showed themselves early. By the time he was six years old, his mother had him singing in the church choir she directed. At nine, he was entering talent contests, and by the time he was eleven, he had won a contest. In an interview with *Teen People*, Usher looked back on that day with pride: "I was a middle-school student and I won a high-school talent competition."

Usher had every reason to feel proud of his talent. His mother was as proud as he was; she knew that his talent was unusual, the sort that could take him far in life. But Chattanooga didn't offer a lot of musical opportunities—so J-Pat moved herself and her sons to Atlanta, Georgia, where she hoped to be able to connect Usher with the musical possibilities he deserved.

Once the family had settled in Atlanta, J-Pat got a job as choir director at a Baptist church—and Usher continued to sing in the church choir. By the time he was twelve, he was part of a local R&B group called NuBeginnings. And his mother made sure he kept entering every talent show he could.

The Hip-Hop Scene

During Usher's childhood, a new kind of music arrived on the scene. Born of a long musical history that included **Gospel**, rhythm and blues, and **funk**, the earliest hip-hop music rapped out its rhythms in the streets of the South Bronx in New York City. In the 1970s, hip-hop was a **subculture** that belonged only to inner-city young people.

But as Usher grew up, so did hip-hop. As he became a teenager, hip-hop's rhythm was going mainstream. Hip-hop record companies were looking for new artists to help them spread the beat.

Usher's music career began by singing in church choirs directed by his mother, J-Pat. Today, Usher, his mother, and younger brother James remain close. In this photo, J-Pat and James are shown at the launch party for Usher's "Truth Tour."

Fame Comes Early

At one of the talent shows he entered, Usher met Bryan Reid, the brother of L.A. Reid from LaFace Records. Bryan was impressed with Usher's talent, and he wanted his brother to meet him. In 1992, when Usher was still only fourteen years old, he auditioned for LaFace Records.

The record **executives** liked what they heard. Usher signed a contract with their record label. His career was rolling now!

As so often happens, one success led to another. The following year, Usher went on the television show *Star Search*. He won in his category and received the award for Best Teen Male Vocalist. He also made music history when he won the record for the longest-held note sung by a child (12.1 seconds).

Winning on *Star Search* brought Usher to the attention of still more people in the music industry. He was asked to perform a song for the soundtrack of the movie *Poetic Justice*, which starred Janet Jackson. Later the same year, that song—"Call Me a Mack"—became Usher's first single.

Puff Daddy

By 1994, Usher was hard at work on his first album for LaFace Records. The album was titled *Usher*, and the album's **producer** was one of the biggest names in the hip-hop world: Sean "Puffy" Combs, known at the time as Puff Daddy (better known now as P. Diddy).

Puffy brought Usher to live with him in New York City while they made the album. The older musician and the young one enjoyed working together. Puffy later told *People* magazine: "Usher became like a little brother to me. I got to see all of his talents. Usher's easy to work with, he listens, he's an incredible singer and an excellent dancer."

Facing Challenges

Usher was honored to work with Puff Daddy. But the man and the boy didn't always agree on the direction Usher's career should take. Usher felt Puffy was trying to turn him into something he wasn't—a sullen, somber rebel who wasn't the real Usher. Puff Daddy made the young boy look like a tough guy, and the explicit lyrics on his album earned Usher the disapproval of some critics. Usher told *People* magazine: "It was the wrong direction, that whole bad-boy thing. Cool guys smile. Cool guys can be sexy."

While he was working on his first album, Usher lived with Sean "Puff Daddy" Combs (together again in this 2002 photo), probably the most influential music producer of the time. Though they didn't agree on everything, it was a learning time for the sixteen-year-old musician.

Usher and Puffy ran into another problem as well, one they hadn't expected: in the middle of recording the album, Usher's voice changed! He told *Teen People* this "was the most tragic thing that has ever happened to me." The voice that had always served him so skillfully and reliably now seemed to belong to someone else. He didn't know how to control it anymore. When he tried to hit the high notes that had once come so easily, his voice cracked or disappeared.

Usher wasn't always comfortable with the image Puff Daddy was carving for him in the music world. To Usher, the "bad-boy" image just wasn't his style, and he wasn't comfortable with the explicit words in some of the songs Puff Daddy wanted him to perform.

Several voice coaches helped Usher with his singing during this period of his life, but Usher still felt as though he were being rejected. "Instead of having support from certain people who I believed in," he told *Teen People*, "they turned away and just didn't believe in me." To add insult to injury, his skin was suddenly covered with pimples. "His whole face just broke out because he was so nervous," J-Pat told *Teen People*. His entire body seemed to be betraying him!

Being a teenager is difficult enough, but given that Usher was away from home, facing new challenges, trying to establish a career, and dealing with all the normal frustrations of being an adolescent, all at the same time, it's no wonder he felt discouraged and uncertain. But Usher didn't give up. He struggled through his voice problems, his embarrassment, and his uncertainty. In 1994, his album *Usher* was released.

What's Next?

A single from *Usher*, "Think of You," made the top ten on the music charts. Eventually, it even went **gold** and sold more than 500,000 copies. But even with a hit single to his name, Usher had trouble knowing where to go next.

Usher could easily have thought that once he managed to actually get his album out, his musical career would just fall magically into place. But that's not the way things turned out. Record executives weren't impressed by the album's overall sales. Meanwhile, Puff Daddy was too busy with his own career to have much time to help Usher.

Usher was still only sixteen years old. He had to finish high school back home in Georgia. He was also interested in an acting career. His mom wasn't about to give up on her son's career—and neither was he.

The late 1990s were busy for Usher. He recorded albums, contributed songs to movie soundtracks and an Olympic tribute album, recorded holiday commercials for Coke, and went on his first tour. Oh, and he graduated from high school, too.

2

His Way

Usher's first album may not have been a groundbreaking success—but it did help to bring him to the attention of the musical world. Now that he had learned how to manage his new grown-up voice, his singing was in demand as much as ever. Usher's career wasn't established yet—but he found himself facing many new opportunities.

Singing Songs

Later the same year his album was released, he contributed to the soundtrack of a movie called *Jason's Lyric*, which starred Jada Pinkett. The soundtrack included a song called "U Will Know," which was performed by several other male singers, as well as Usher, all singing together as Black Men United. The next year, his friend Monica, a popular singer, asked Usher to sing with her on the song "Let's Straighten It Out." And later that year, he recorded holiday commercial jingles for the Coca-Cola company. He also contributed a song to the 1996 Olympics' **tribute** album, *Rhythm of the Games*.

Usher was definitely keeping busy. He wasn't so busy with his music, though, that he didn't follow through with his education. With the support of a tutor who helped him make up for his many absences from school, Usher graduated from high school.

The Next Album

LaFace Records decided to give Usher another chance, even though his first album had not sold as well as they had hoped. In 1996, the record company asked three of hip-hop's biggest producers—Babyface, Teddy Riley, and Jermaine Dupri—to work with Usher on his new album.

These three men were at the top of their careers—but they were willing to listen to Usher's ideas as well. Usher told his fans on his official Web site: "What we ended up writing and recording was about my life—about what I've dealt with, being a teenager who's going into manhood." Usher cowrote six of the album's nine songs, proving that he had musical talents besides singing.

In 1997, Usher's second album—*My Way*—was released. It included the **ballad** "Bed Time," which Babyface had produced, and Monica recorded a new duet with Usher, "Slow Jam." Teddy Riley produced another ballad for the album, and Jermaine Dupri did his share as well. In fact, Dupri's songs would make Usher's name.

Dupri's songs—"You Make Me Wanna . . ." and "Nice and Slow"—climbed the music charts all the way to the top. In the end, "You Make Me Wanna . . ." went **platinum** and spent fourteen weeks in the number-one position on the *Billboard* R&B and pop music charts. A year later, *My Way* was 1998's eleventh best-selling album—and Usher's success had finally arrived. All of a sudden, he was one of hip-hop's hottest young musicians.

Recognition

The years 1997 and 1998 were amazing for Usher, as awards and recognitions rolled in one after another. He was named 1998's Billboard Entertainer of the Year. *Teen People* chose him as one of the "21 Hottest Stars Under 21." He won a Soul Train Music Award for Best R&B/Soul Single for "You Make Me Wanna . . .", and he even got a Grammy nomination for Best Male R&B Vocal Performance for his album's title song, "My Way."

In 1996, Usher had the chance to work with another of hip-hop's superstar producers and writers, Jermaine Dupri (shown here with Usher in 2004). Jermaine's songs finally brought Usher the success he had worked for since childhood.

The next year, 1999, was just as good for Usher. He recorded a song with Mariah Carey (who was the biggest-selling artist of the 1990s), and their song, "How Much," was featured on her hit album, *Rainbow*. That same year, Usher's live album and video, *Usher Live*, was released. Both were recorded during a free concert Usher performed in his childhood town of Chattanooga, Tennessee.

Going On Tour

In 1997, Usher realized the time had come for him to get both himself and his music out to his fans. And if he was going to be out in the public eye, he needed a more polished image. Although he was already an accomplished dancer, a **choreographer** helped him make his moves even more smooth and exciting. He lost some weight and created a

Usher toured for the first time in 1997. A choreographer worked with him to polish his dancing, and he opened for Puff Daddy, Mary J. Blige, and Janet Jackson. Crowds everywhere wildly greeted the new star.

sexy new look for himself. By the time he performed live at the Apollo Theater in September 1997, he was ready—and the audience agreed!

In November of the same year, Usher launched a tour to back up his albums. He **opened** for Puff Daddy's No Way Out tour through early 1998, and then signed on as Mary J. Blige's opening act. By July, he was opening for Janet Jackson's Velvet Rope tour.

The Risks of Fame

Usher loves performing for live audiences, but he sometimes experiences a little stage fright. When that happens, he has a trick for handling his nervousness: "I get ten bags of M&Ms and spill them on a table," he told *J-14* magazine. "Then I sort them out into little piles of all the same color. It takes a while but it does the trick!"

Knowing that he's done all he can to prepare for his shows also helps Usher stay calm. He spends hours and hours making sure his performances are as exciting as they can possibly be. He studies the dance moves of other dancers he admires, including the old-time dancers like Fred Astaire and Gene Kelly, as well as hot, modern dancers like Michael Jackson. Usher told *USA Today*, "I study Gene Kelly for the grace, the shoulders, the posture."

Dancing is strenuous physical exercise, so Usher has to work hard at staying in shape. Rehearsals can be exhausting—and dangerous! During a rehearsal for his 1999 tour to Australia and New Zealand, he dislocated his shoulder and ended up having to cancel the concerts. Usher told *J-14*, "Bungee jumping would be light compared to this industry. It's sort of like jumping off a bridge without a parachute."

Live performances can be risky in other ways as well. For instance, while Usher was performing in England in 1998, someone in the audience opened a can of tear gas. Usher was all right—he hadn't even reached the stage yet—but a few fans had to be hospitalized. Usher has learned to be careful of his security. He told *People* magazine that in large crowds, "People have to dress up as me and be **decoys**."

Even when the fans are friendly, being so famous carries its own stress. Wherever Usher goes, people recognize him—even when he goes to the bathroom! "I'm in the stall, and this guy is on the phone and I can hear his conversation," Usher told *Twist* magazine. "He's talking to his sister, saying, "He's in the stall right next to me!"

Though fans can be just a bit overenthusiastic sometimes, Usher likes to meet and talk with them when possible. In this 1998 photo, Usher is talking to a fan during a stop on his tour as the opening act for Janet Jackson.

So much public attention can make a person uncomfortable! And the chance of making a big mistake when you're in public is one of the risks of being famous. Usher won a Grammy nomination in 1997—but at the awards telecast, while an international television watched, he made a big blooper and introduced award-winner and rock legend Bob Dylan as "Bill."

Television to Big Screen

These were busy years for Usher. At the same time that he was promoting his music career with tours, he was also breaking into acting. He made his acting **debut** on the television show *Moesha,* which starred pop singer Brandy, as Moesha's boyfriend, Jeremy.

Usher proved he had acting ability, and he was offered guest appearances on a couple of TV series: *Promised Land* and *The Parent 'Hood.* In June 1998, he did such a good job in eight episodes of the daytime soap opera *The Bold and the Beautiful* that a year later, the NAACP gave him the Image Award for Outstanding Actor in a Daytime Drama Series. (The NAACP, an organization that works for equal rights for African Americans, gives these awards to performers who create positive images of black Americans.)

The same year that Usher made his debut as a soap opera star, he also broke into movies. His first movie role was in the science fiction thriller *The Faculty,* where Usher played a high school student possessed by aliens; actor Elijah Wood, of *Lord of the Rings* fame, also starred in the movie. The following year, Usher had a minor role as a DJ in *She's All That,* which starred Freddie Prinze Jr. and Rachael Leigh Cook. Later that year, he also costarred with Vanessa Williams in *Light It Up,* which was produced by Babyface. Usher played a teenager working to improve his rundown high school.

The film's producers were convinced from the beginning that Usher could handle the challenges he would face in his first starring role in a major motion picture. "Usher just explodes with **charisma,**" producer Kenny Edmonds told Fox Movies. Edmonds, who had been working on music projects with the young star for several years, went on to say:

"He has such confidence in everything he does. Usher is a very hard worker; he gives everything 200 percent as a singer. So I expected nothing less from him as an actor."

Producer Craig Bolotin agreed:

"Usher turned out to be a real actor and not a singer who's moonlighting as an actor. He was very committed to the film and to understanding his role. Lester is

a difficult part, but Usher really got the character and played it beautifully."

Usher, for his part, was excited by the new opportunities the role offered him. He told Fox Movies:

"I've always loved music, but there's so much more to being an entertainer than singing and dancing. To be a triple threat you have to have the acting. So I figured I'll take the step. And *Light It Up* gave me the chance to really get into it."

Usher liked the role he played; he felt Lester was a complex and sympathetic figure.

"For someone so young, Lester is carrying an awful lot. He's had a difficult and challenging life, dealing with family issues or the problems of his friends at school. Lester has a very open heart; he's very caring and giving."

The producers of *Light It Up* asked Usher to record a song for the soundtrack—but Usher said no. He told *Entertainment Weekly*, "I wanted to be taken seriously as an actor." In other words, he didn't want people to think he was in the movie simply because of his musical skills.

Usher's two careers—acting and music—sometimes conflicted with each other. He simply didn't have time for everything. Because of scheduling difficulties with shooting *Light It Up* at the same time that he was performing as the opening act for Janet Jackson's Velvet Rope tour, he finally had to give up his act on the tour. It must have been a difficult decision to make, but Usher felt he had done the right thing. "I'm happy that I had a chance to show myself as an actor," he told the *San Francisco Chronicle*.

Now that he had proved what he could do as an actor, roles kept coming his way. In 1999, he costarred in *Texas Rangers* with James Van Der Beek, Dylan McDermott, and Rachael Leigh Cook. The 2000 film tells the story of a group of young people who fight to protect the West in the years after the Civil War. This movie offered Usher a few

Usher broke into acting in 1997. His first role was as Jeremy, Moesha's boyfriend on the television series of the same name. The title character was played by Brandy, another top musical talent. This was just the beginning of Usher's acting career.

Usher learned to ride a horse for the film *Texas Rangers,* the story of young people who band together to protect the West after the Civil War. The film stars (left to right) Ashton Kutcher, James Van Der Beek, Dylan McDermott, and Usher.

new challenges: for instance, he had to learn to ride a horse. He told MTV, "I got a few sores, you know, blisters from riding on those horses. Saddles are hard when you're not used to them."

Meanwhile, Usher's face was still being seen regularly on television as well. He had TV appearances on the Billboard Music Awards, VIBE-TV, *The Keenan Ivory Wayans Show*, *Live with Regis & Kathie Lee*, *The Oprah Winfrey Show*, *The Chris Rock Show*, Dick Clark's *New Year's Rockin' Eve*, UNICEF's *Gift Of Song*, and Nickelodeon's *Big Help-a-Thon* and *All That*.

His Own Record Label

In 1998, Usher expanded his career in yet another way: he created his own record label, Us Records. Puerto Rican singer Melinda Santiago was one of the first musicians he signed. Usher was excited to have the opportunity to use all he had learned to help other up-and-coming musicians.

Moving Ahead

By 1999, Usher was twenty-one years old—and he had already accomplished more than many people do in a lifetime. He had earned riches and recognition for his talent—and he had become a well-known public figure as well. Politicians even courted his approval; in November 1999, he and basketball star Kareem Abdul Jabbar and tennis pro John McEnroe took part in a fundraiser at Madison Square Garden in New York City for Democratic presidential hopeful and former senator Bill Bradley.

Life was going well for Usher. He was doing it his way—and his way was going just fine for him.

But there was plenty more success still to come.

Usher's overwhelming success of the 1990s continued into the new century. The new millennium brought new music and acting opportunities for the superstar. Usher's 2001 album *8701* showed his fans and critics how much he had matured musically and personally.

3

Big Ush

As Usher went into his twenties, he was like a juggler tossing balls at a frantic pace—and never dropping one. Dancing, singing, acting, producing, and running his own business: there simply seemed to be no end to feats Usher could pull off! His energy and his success earned him the nicknames "Big Ush" and "Big Tyme." In the hip-hop world, he was truly big—and he had certainly made the big time!

False Start

Early in 2001, Usher was all set to release another album, which would have been titled *All About U*, when he discovered that tracks from the album had been leaked to Napster, the Internet's music-sharing service. Arista, Usher's CD company, decided to delay the album's release. Usher was frustrated—but his creative energy was still seething. The delay gave him the chance to go back to the recording studio and create fresh new songs for the album.

8701

Later in 2001, Usher's fourth album was released; this time around it was titled *8701*. (Get it? It was released August 7, 2001. The numbers also represent the years that Usher had been in the music business, from 1987 to 2001.) The album proved that Usher was growing as an artist, rather than just depending on what had worked for him in the past. In *8701*, he spread his wings and tried some new things. "I really analyzed myself as an artist and I'm really like a rapper who sings," he said at the time, according to the Magic Web site. "I like to tell stories in my songs. . . . I did a lot of writing this time. It was like an evolution and I was involved conceptually this time with every tune."

The album proved that Usher was no "flash in the pan," a speck of gold that would be gone before long. Usher had worked hard to create music that would show he was a man now, no longer just a superstar kid. "The album is really about my evolution as an artist, as a writer, as a producer and as a man," he told IMDb.com. "I learned how music works dealing with Jermaine Dupri, and I learned how image works dealing with Puff Daddy." *8701* showcased both Usher's music and his image, demonstrating that he had absorbed what both his **mentors** had offered him—and combined it with the talent that was uniquely his own. The singles that were released from the album helped build Usher's reputation as they climbed the hit lists.

Released even before the album, "Pop Ya Collar," produced and cowritten by Kevin "She'kespere" Briggs, showed that Usher's appeal reached beyond the United States. When the song was released in Europe, it became a number-two hit in the United Kingdom.

"U Remind Me" was the album's first advance single back home in the United States. The song, produced by Philadelphia's Edmund "Eddie Hustle" Clement, had a tough, addictive beat that was woven together with an R&B-flavored melody. Exactly a month before the album's release, "U Remind Me" **simultaneously** hit the number-one spot on both the pop and the R&B lists—and it stayed at the top of both charts for four weeks.

The album's other songs were also successful. A month after the album's release, "U Got It Bad," a slow **jam** written by Usher, Dupri, and Brian Cox, was number one on the pop list for six weeks and the

Usher wasn't just a superstar in the United States. His song "Pop Ya Collar" was a major hit in Europe and a number-two hit in the United Kingdom. In this 2001 photo, Usher is performing at the Music of Black Origin Awards in London.

number-one R&B song for seven weeks. "U Don't Have to Call," one of two **tracks** on the album that the Neptunes produced, kept Usher on the singles charts into 2002 when it reached number two on the R&B list and number three on the pop. By the time "Can U Help Me"

The album *8701* made Usher part of music history. Songs from that album won Usher the Best Male R&B Vocal Grammys in consecutive years. Usher is only the third artist to win the award back to back.

(a **collaboration** with hit-makers Jimmy Jam and Terry Lewis) was released as the fourth single from *8701* in late-summer 2002, the album had gone platinum four times.

"U Remind Me" won the Best Male R&B Vocal Award at the Grammy ceremonies in February 2002. In 2003, Usher made Grammy history when his single "U Got It Bad," also from *8701*, won the same award—Best Male R&B Vocal—at the ceremonies one year later. This made Usher the only artist besides Luther Vandross (more than a decade before) and Stevie Wonder (back in the 1970s) to win that award in two consecutive years.

Keeping Creative

Usher was busy during these years. As he watched the songs from *8701* climb the charts, he was still creating new work. He and Loon joined Usher's old mentor Puff Daddy (but by this time, he was known as P. Diddy) on a song called "I Need a Girl"—which turned into a run-away number-two pop and number-two R&B hit, spending a half year on the charts.

For Usher, the year 2002 closed out with an interesting trio of dramatic television series opportunities, all in November. He appeared on *The Twilight Zone*, *7th Heaven*, and Dick Clark's *American Dreams* (where Usher portrayed music legend Marvin Gaye).

The year that followed, 2003, would be a full and fulfilling one for Usher. But 2004 was the year when he truly exploded around the globe, thanks to his chart-topping single "Yeah" (produced by Lil Jon). The song (and Usher's album *Confessions*) shot Usher straight up into the highest levels of music superstardom.

Released in 2004, *Confessions* is perhaps Usher's most personal album. His songs talk about his relationships with his family, people in the music business, and with fame. On this album, Usher doesn't sugarcoat his life; he tells it like it is.

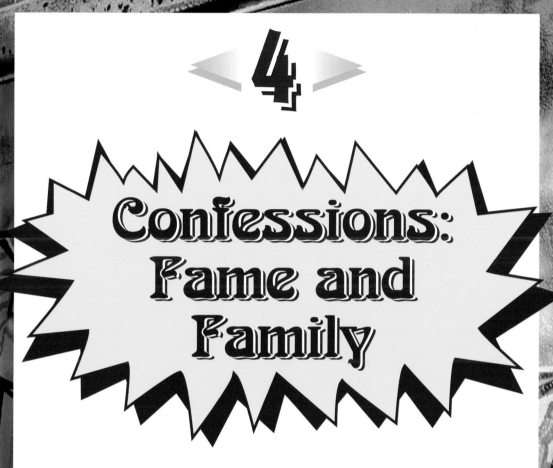

4

Confessions: Fame and Family

Usher's next album, *Confession*, not only brought him fame; it also proved he wasn't afraid to openly face difficult personal issues. He told Magic.com, "I'm twenty-five years old, and I'm dealing with my responsibilities as a man and I'm not afraid to speak, to be realistic and talk about the issues men deal with. I'm telling on myself."

More than one song on the album dealt with the mix of honesty and dishonesty that is so often found in relationships. Few other musicians had tried to tackle such weighty and personal material—but Usher was growing up. He had come a long way in his career, but he understood that relationships are as important as fame.

Family Relationships

Usher has close ties to his family. He and his younger half-brother, James, have a good relationship, and Usher is also close to his extended family, his grandparents, aunts and uncles, and cousins. But his closest family relationship has always been with his mother. She was the one who first taught him about music and singing, and she was the one who helped him get his career started. She gave him support all through the early difficult years of his career, and her encouragement continued to be important to him as he grew older and became successful. "She's always been there for me," he told the Associated Press. "It always helps to have someone behind you, and my mother was that person."

But although Usher's mother has always played a major role in his life, he lacked a father figure in his life while he was growing up. When he was in his early teens, his mother and Usher's stepfather, Terry Patton, were divorced. Usher Raymond III, the star's father, had not been involved in his son's life after he separated from J-Pat. In fact, Usher didn't see his father until his grandmother's funeral, fifteen years after his parents' separation. Usher never formed a sense of connection with his father. He told *Teen People* that he wasn't sorry about this. "I don't have any remorse," he said, "because I've never had a relationship with him. How can you love somebody or hate somebody you've never known?"

Almost Like Family

Usher's music career brought benefits to him that went far beyond money and fame. L.A. Reid from LaFace Records became a stand-in male role model for the young star. Usher told *USA Today*, "L.A. took me under his wing like a father." Puff Daddy also provided Usher with a replacement father figure. Each man helped guide Usher as he grew professionally: L.A. Reid taught Usher about older music styles and performers, like the Dells and the Spinners. Puff Daddy helped Usher understand the ins and outs of music production.

Girlfriends

Usher's *Confessions* makes clear that Usher's romantic life has not always been easy. But then, few romantic lives are!

Usher's earliest interest in the opposite sex was sometimes embarrassing and painful. He told *Twist*, "I was at the skating rink

In this 2005 photo, Usher and his mother are attending the premiere of *In the Mix*. J-Pat has been a major influence on Usher's career and life. She taught him music, encouraged him to compete in talent shows, supporting him every step of the way.

Dating hasn't always been easy for Usher. In 2004, he dated model Naomi Campbell, a superstar in her own right (seen here at the 2004 MTV European Music Awards). According to sources, they broke up when she refused to attend the *Billboard* awards.

and I grabbed a girl by the arm because she refused to skate with me. I wanted to hold hands, but she ran off and left me hanging." He also described his first breakup: "We were moving to Atlanta, so I had to break up with her. The situation broke my heart. And nobody ever knew it—but I cried and cried."

As an adult, Usher's romantic relationships continued to have their ups and downs. From 2002 through 2004, he dated Rozonda "Chilli" Thomas (a member of TLC), but their relationship came to a stormy end when she accused him of cheating on her. In the fall of 2004, Usher started dating supermodel Naomi Campbell. The couple appeared together often socially and at awards ceremonies, but once again Usher ran into romantic problems. According to superiorpics.com, one of Usher's friends said:

> **Things came to a head at the Billboard Awards when she told him she wasn't going with him and he got all tetchy with her. He went in the back door. That probably wouldn't have happened if Naomi had been there.**

Usher described the pain of breaking up in an interview with VH1:

> **You've gotten attached, you love that person. You spent the utmost respect, time and dedication to try to create a comfortable relationship for that person. It didn't work, so it burns.**

Usher's song "Burn" on his *Confessions* album described this pain in detail. He told VH1 that the song was **autobiographical** in many ways.

> **No one can really explain that gut-wrenching feeling you feel when you're going through it, when you figured, 'I thought that this was my soul mate. I thought I found the person who had it and I thought I could be that person, too.' You've gotta go through something to get to something sometimes. My mom always said, 'If there were no humps in life, there would be nothing to get over.'**

Shaking His Fears

Confessions described Usher's personal heartaches—but clearly, listeners related to both the lyrics and the music. His honesty and his talent combined to create a sound that everyone loved.

"With every album, I try to better myself," Usher said before the album's release, according to Magic.com.

> **"I'm a perfectionist and with the success of my last record [*8701*], I wasn't sure about where my growth should be—as a performer, as a vocalist. I always felt like I held something back on my albums— on every album, I was playing a 'role.' This time, I decided to shake my fears and allow my personality to come through."**

Apparently, Usher's personality shone as bright as his talent. The album's success was phenomenal.

Record-Breaker

Released in March 2004, *Confessions* sold a record-breaking 1.1 million units in its first week out. Usher now had his first number-one hit on the *Billboard* 200 Albums chart; at the same time, he had his first simultaneous number-one pop and number-one R&B single. The CD dominated the album charts throughout the year. In the end, it spent a total of twelve weeks at number one, while it spun off three number-one hit singles: "Yeah!" (featuring Lil' Jon and Ludacris), "Burn," and "Confessions Part II."

The album's performance broke record after record. It not only had the highest first-week numbers ever scanned by a male R&B artist in Soundscan's thirteen-year history (breaking R. Kelly's record back in 2000), but it also had the highest first-week sales by any male artist since Eminem's *Marshall Mathers* (also in 2000). Usher's success also marked the biggest debut week in the thirty years of the Arista label's existence, breaking the record held since 1997 by Notorious B.I.G.

Confessions broke other long-standing chart records as well:

- It had the highest sales for overall R&B debut in the Soundscan era, passing Destiny's Child's *Survivor* in May 2001.

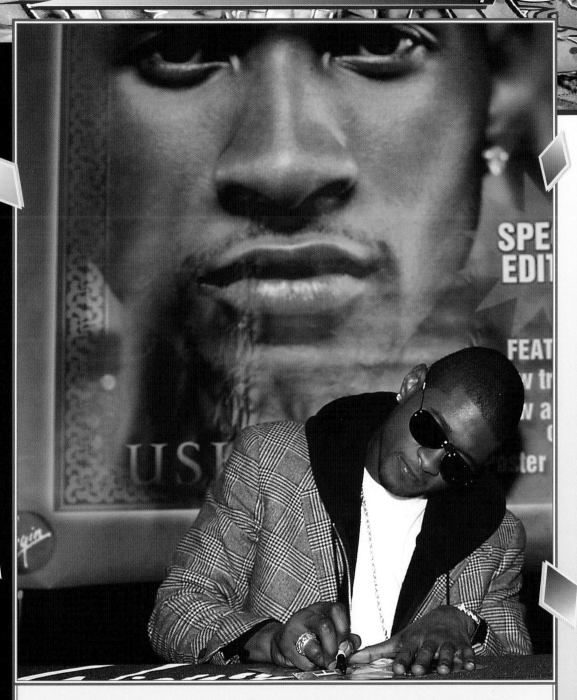

Confessions spent twelve weeks at the top spot on the charts. Three number-one solo singles came from that album. Sales during the first week topped one million copies! Here, Usher is seen signing copies of a special edition of the record-breaker.

- It had the highest sales for solo R&B debut in the Soundscan era, surpassing Alicia Keys' *Songs in A Minor* in June 2001.

- It had the highest single-week sales in Arista history, surpassing the second week of *The Bodyguard* soundtrack in December 1992.

- It had the highest overall debut sales of 2004, surpassing Norah Jones' *Feels Like Home* in February.

By May 1, 2004, when Usher appeared as the musical guest on NBC's *Saturday Night Live*, Soundscan sales were past 3 million. Later that month, the BET Awards released their list of nominations, and Usher was named in four categories, all for the single "Yeah!": Best Male R&B Artist, Video of the Year, Best Collaboration, and Viewers' Choice. Two days later, the chart news was just as amazing: Usher became only the third lead artist in pop music history (the other two were the Beatles in 1964 and the Bee Gees in 1978)—and the first solo artist ever to have three singles in the top ten on the Hot 100. Usher was still making history.

At the June 29th BET Awards telecast (with *Confessions* now past 4 million sales), Usher won the Best Male R&B Artist Award and "Yeah!" won the Viewers' Choice. Two months later, on August 29, Usher interrupted his sold-out North American tour (with Kanye West and Christina Milian) to pick up the first two MTV VMAs of his career: Best Male Video and Best Dance Video.

On September 16, the World Music Awards, broadcast on the ABC network in the United States, recognized Usher's achievement. He walked away with Best Male Artist, Best Male Pop Artist, and Best R&B Artist. *Confessions* had now moved past the 5 million mark.

The album was so successful that seven months after its first release, a deluxe repackaged, redesigned, limited-edition version of the album (with a 3-D cover and fold-out poster inside the jewel case) was released. *Confessions (Special Edition)* also included four bonus tracks. One of these turned out to be a fourth number-one pop and a number-one R&B hit single: "My Boo," an electrifying duet with J Records artist Alicia Keys that was produced by Jermaine Dupri for So So Def Productions and coproduced by Manuel Seal. Chris Robinson directed the video on location in New York City.

teenVOGUE

beauty flash
brown hair is back

avril+usher
style superstars

THE SHAPE ISSUE
- what to wear if you're CURVY, SHORT, TALL, ATHLETIC
- 10 ways to feel great about your body
- PLUS food for thought—what's in your lunch?

JEWELRY RULES!
pile on the new bling

SCHOOL STRESS
how to deal

Confessions' success was nothing short of phenomenal. The album was hot, and so was Usher. Everybody wanted Usher—television shows, films, magazines. He even posed with singer Avril Lavigne on the November 2004 cover of fashion magazine *Teen Vogue.*

On Tuesday, October 5, 2004, a special event was arranged at the Virgin Megastore on Union Square in New York City. A limited number of fans who had prepaid for *Confessions (Special Edition)* on the Friday before stood in line for their copy of the album. They had been given exclusive passes to meet Usher at the store on Monday night, and excitement was high.

The special edition of *Confessions* contained additional tracks, including a duet with fellow superstar Alicia Keys. "My Boo" became the fourth number-one hit from that album. Usher and Alicia performed the song in London in November 2004.

And no wonder. Usher's awards just kept coming. Six days later, at the annual Source Hip-Hop Music Awards in Miami on October 11, "Yeah!" won as the R&B/Rap Collaboration of the Year, and Usher was named Male R&B Artist of the Year. The same month but an ocean away, Usher was named Top Male Artist at the first annual Nordic Music Awards broadcast on October 2. The next night, at the Aladdin Hotel-Casino back in Las Vegas, Usher picked up three Radio Music Awards, as he was named Artist of the Year for Hip Hop/Rhythmic Radio and Cingular Artist of the Year. Meanwhile, "Yeah!" won as Song of the Year for Hip-Hop/Rhythmic Radio.

But the awards season wasn't over yet for 2004. On November 15 at the ABC network telecast of the 32nd annual American Music Awards, Usher won all four categories in which he was nominated, including Favorite Male Artist and Favorite Album (*Confessions*) in both the Pop/Rock and Soul/R&B categories. Four nights later at the MTV Europe EMAs in Rome, Usher added two more awards to his stash, for Best Male and Best Album. The only thing left for 2004, was the Billboard Music Awards, where Usher walked away with another eleven trophies, including Artist of the Year, Album of the Year, and Hot 100 Single of the Year (for "Yeah!").

At this point in his life, Usher had already been in the music business for a decade. Now he was poised to begin his second decade as a recording megastar. But he still wasn't satisfied with developing his talents in just one area.

Building His Acting Career

While Usher was producing musically, he was also proving his flexibility as an actor. He acted and sang in the TV musical *Geppetto,* which aired on ABC's *Wonderful World of Disney* on May 7, 2000. The movie was based on the Pinocchio story and starred Drew Carey; Usher played the singing Ring Leader on Pleasure Island. He told MTV, "The Pinocchio story was something I loved as a kid, and I though it was really creative of Disney to do it from the father's perspective."

In 2000, Usher played another role for Disney. This time he went to Toronto to film the Disney Channel's season opener for the series *The Famous Jett Jackson.* Showing again his flexibility as an actor, Usher played an evil skateboarder and computer hacker.

Usher continues to flex his acting skills. In 2005, he costarred with Chazz Palminteri in *In the Mix*. Usher played a nightclub DJ who saves the life of a mob boss (Palminteri). He's then hired to protect the boss's daughter. Usher also coproduced the film.

Usher's biggest acting opportunity came with the movie *In the Mix*. Released in 2005, the movie tells the story of a nightclub DJ (Usher) who saves the life of a mob boss—and is rewarded for his bravery with the responsibility of watching the don's beautiful daughter (Emmanuelle Chriqui). The romantic sparks fly between the DJ and the daughter, despite the fact that they come from very different worlds. After the ups and downs of falling in love in the midst of the mob world, the romantic comedy ends happily. It was directed by Ron Underwood and produced by John Dellaverson; the film's executive producers included Bill Borden, Holly DavisCarter, Michael Paseornek—and Usher himself.

The Godson of Soul

At the beginning of 2004, Usher told *People* magazine that his New Year's resolution was "to slow down and breathe, because you must find balance in the middle of **mayhem**." Finding time to breathe may have been hard for Usher during 2004, and yet somehow he was able to keep his balance.

After all Usher had accomplished, some artists might have been ready to relax and take it easy. But Usher was still going strong. After he danced on stage with funk superstar James Brown at the 2005 Grammys, Brown crowned him "Godson of Soul." Usher was walking toward the future in the footsteps of music's greatest names. And not only was he accomplishing great things musically, he was also doing his part to make the world a better place.

Usher has often said he wants to make a difference. His foundation, Usher's New Look, brings a variety of programs to disadvantaged children and adults. It's just one way Usher has found to reach out to others.

‹5›

Dreams and Goals

Usher told *Rolling Stone*: "My goal is to be successful and to change music and to make a difference." Clearly, he's already reached the first of those goals, and he's working on the second and third. The originality of his music is changing the way people look at hip-hop—and his charity work makes a big difference in the world.

Reaching Out to Others

One of Usher's biggest dreams is to be able to give inner-city kids the same opportunities that he had when he was growing up. "A lot of negativity comes through life for a lot of minorities," he told *Rolling Stone*. "I try to be positive and I try to act as positive role model." To help encourage and inspire these at-risk kids, Usher hosted a three-day fan club convention back in April 1999. The convention included a talent contest and fashion show, as well as guest appearances from Puff Daddy, Jermaine Dupri, and members of the Atlanta Falcons football team. But that was just the beginning for

Usher. He went on to produce regular talent shows in his hometown of Atlanta, Georgia. He told MTV, "I'm more or less trying to do something positive for kids who live in the inner city."

As part of this goal, Usher participated in the NBA's Stay in School program, which works to help young people understand how important education is to their success in life. A big basketball fan (as of March 2005, Usher is even part owner of his own team, the Cleveland Cavaliers), Usher enjoyed the chance to hook up with the NBA. 'N Sync's Challenge for the Children benefit game at Georgia State University gave him the chance to shoot some hoops himself—and raise money for children's charities. Mase, Kobe Bryant, and the 'N Sync guys joined Usher on the court. In August 2002, Usher had the chance to play some basketball again when he participated in the 17th Annual Magic Johnson "A Midsummer Night's Magic" celebrity basketball game, a charity event that benefits a scholarship fund. The next year, Usher performed with a group of kids at the NBA's All-Star Jam Session, a "Read to Achieve" celebration that encouraged kids to get involved with books and reading.

Usher was also the national spokesperson for the U.S. Department of Transportation's Get Big on Safety campaign. And when he's home in Atlanta, he spends time at the Boys & Girls Club. Usher is grateful to the organization for giving him a place to go after school when he was young. "Every chance I get," he told the Associated Press, "I sit down with the kids and talk to them. I tell them, 'Do what you've got to do to succeed. I'm always going to encourage you.'"

Usher is always reaching out to others in whatever ways he can, as often as he can. After September 11, 2001, he did his part to raise money for the families of the victims of the terrorist attacks on America. Along with many other stars, he performed at the "United We Stand" benefit concert in Washington, D.C. In 2002, he performed at the HIV/AIDS awareness concert "Staying Alive" in Cape Town, South Africa. HIV and AIDS kills more people in Africa than all the other natural disasters combined, and Usher wanted to do his part to call attention to this terrible problem. The concert also featured six South African musicians, as well as Usher's old friends P. Diddy and Alicia Keys. The concert was played globally on MTV on December 1, World AIDS Day. Three years later, Usher and Alicia Keys joined up again on behalf of HIV/AIDS victims. This time, they performed at the "Black Ball," an annual event that Alicia Keys hosts

Usher is a huge basketball fan, and in March 2005, he fulfilled a dream he shares with many NBA fans—he bought part of a team, the Cleveland Cavaliers. He also participates in many NBA charity events, including "Read to Achieve."

to raise money for Keep a Child Alive, an organization that works to provide treatments in developing countries to children and families affected by HIV or AIDS.

Hurricane Relief

After hurricanes Katrina and Rita hit America's Gulf Coast region, Usher stepped up to the plate to do his part in the relief effort. He started Project Restart, which was kicked off with a benefit concert for the hurricane victims on October 9 in Atlanta, Georgia. Usher performed several songs at the concert, and some of his celebrity friends made special guest appearances. With the help of corporate sponsors such as Hibernia Bank, Visa, and SunTrust Bank, as well as leaders like Atlanta's mayor Shirley Franklin, Usher invited five thousand Katrina and Rita **evacuees** who had relocated to Georgia to attend the concert for free. All proceeds from the concert benefited Project Restart, which worked to provide temporary housing to those who had lost their homes in the hurricanes.

As part of Project Restart, Usher's New Look Foundation teamed up with Freddie Mac with the goal of placing a thousand families in homes in thirteen different states. The proceeds from the benefit concert were used to help Katrina victims settle into their permanent or semi-permanent homes.

On his official Web site Usher World, Usher said:

"When I thought about what I could do to help, I decided that I wanted to do something direct and personal for the evacuees. Their lives have been affected in a major way, so I want to leverage my talents and resources to help bring a sense of joy to those who are in need of a fresh start. This isn't just another concert to benefit the victims . . . this is a movement to uplift the survivors and give them hope."

In 2005, Usher also opened Camp New Look in Atlanta, Georgia. This summer camp for minority youth is designed to help talented kids achieve their dreams. Usher realizes how fortunate his own life has been—and he wants to do his part to continue to pass along that good fortune to young people who are coming up within the black community.

Usher's concern for others is worldwide. In 2002, he, Alicia Keys, and P. Diddy participated in the "Staying Alive" concert in Cape Town, South Africa. Broadcast on World AIDS Day, the goal of the concert was to increase awareness about HIV/AIDS in Africa.

Usher's future seems unlimited. Though he has hinted at early retirement from performing, he shows no sign of letting up anytime soon. Whether it's music, business, film, or charity, there's clearly much more of Usher to come.

Walking the Talk

Some people talk good, but when it comes down to it, they don't live out the things they say they believe. Usher has proven that he lives out his commitment to others—both in public ways and in his private life. In January 2000, while he was driving near Atlanta, he came across a woman who had just escaped from her burning car. Usher pulled off the road beside the accident and did what he could to help. The woman's clothes were on fire, and he used his jacket to smother the flames, then waited with the woman until the ambulance arrived. The woman died from her injuries a few weeks later, but her son was so grateful for what Usher had done that he called a radio station to thank him publicly.

The Future

Because of how strenuous his dance routines are, Usher isn't certain he can keep up the pace of his performances forever. In 2005, he started talking about retiring early, maybe in his forties. But that's still twenty years away—and whether he's dancing and singing on stage, or running businesses and charities, Usher is certain to keep busy. He proved that early in 2006 when he announced he will star in and produce a new film, *The Ballad of Walter Holmes*.

He told E! Online: "This is still just the beginning. . . . I feel like I've accomplished so much already, but I still have my whole life ahead of me and much more to do."

With a career that keeps taking him to new heights of achievement and accomplishment, Usher remains, in his own words, "the master of the moment. I feel like I'm in the prime of my life, physically, emotionally, spiritually—and musically." He further summarized his outlook for the future in an MTV interview: "I'll keep going in the right direction, as long as I keep my head in the sky, keep a positive attitude, and do what I love."

1978   Usher Raymond IV is born in Dallas, Texas, on October 14.

1994   Usher records first album for LaFace Records.

1996   Contributes a song to the 1996 Olympics' tribute album, *Rhythm of the Games.*

1997   Makes his acting debut as Jeremy on *Moesha.*

Receives a Grammy nomination.

Second album, *My Way*, is released.

Performs at the Apollo Theater in New York City.

Tours as opening act on Puff Daddy's No Way Out tour.

1998   Creates his own record label, Us Records.

Makes his film debut as a high school student possessed by aliens in *The Faculty.*

Named Billboard Entertainer of the Year.

Receives a Grammy nomination for Best Male R&B Vocal Performance.

Someone opens a tear gas canister before a concert in England.

Selected one of the "21 Hottest Stars Under 21" by *Teen People.*

Tours as opening act for Mary J. Blige.

Wins Soul Train Music Award for "You Make Me Wanna . . .".

Tours as opening act for Janet Jackson's Velvet Rope tour.

1999   NAACP awards him the Image Award for Outstanding Actor in a Daytime Drama Series in recognition of his work on *The Bold and the Beautiful* in June 1998.

Participates in a fundraiser for Democratic presidential hopeful Bill Bradley.

Records "How Much" with Mariah Carey.

Usher Live, recorded at a free concert in Chattanooga, is released.

Hosts a three-day fan club convention.

2000   Appears in the film *Texas Rangers.*

Films season opener for Disney series *The Famous Jett Jackson.*

Renders aid to a woman who escaped a burning car.

Costars in television special *Geppetto.*

2001 Performs at the "United We Stand" benefit concert in Washington, D.C.

Releases *8701*.

2002 Performs at the "Staying Alive" concert in South Africa.

Wins Best Male R&B Vocal Award at the Grammys.

Participates in the 17th Annual Magic Johnson's "A Midsummer Night's Magic" charity event.

2002 Begins dating Rozonda "Chilli" Thomas of TLC.

2003 Becomes only the third artist to win back to back Grammys as Best Male R&B Vocal.

Performs with a group of kids at the NBA's All-Star Jam Session.

2004 Stops seeing Rozonda "Chilli" Thomas.

Dates model Naomi Campbell.

His album *Confessions* sells a record-breaking 1.1 million in its first week of release, and he has his first simultaneous number-one pop and number-one R&B singles.

Wins eleven Billboard Awards.

Wins Best Male R&B Artist and "Yeah!" wins Viewers' Choice award.

Wins two MTA VMAs.

Wins three World Music Awards.

Wins the Top Male Artist award at the first Nordic Music Awards.

Wins three Radio Music Awards.

Wins two Source Hip-Hop Music Awards.

Wins four American Music Awards.

Wins two MTV Europe EMAs.

2005 Costars in *In the Mix*.

James Brown calls Usher the "Godson of Soul" at the Grammy Awards.

Opens Camp New Look in Atlanta, Georgia.

Performs at the HIV/AIDS benefit, the "Black Ball."

Purchases part ownership of the Cleveland Cavaliers of the NBA.

Starts Project Restart to aid victims of the Gulf Coast hurricanes.

2006 Announces he will star in and produce the film *The Ballad of Walter Holmes*.

Discography
Solo Albums
1994 *Usher*

1997 *My Way*

1999 *Live*

2001 *8701*

2004 *Confessions*

 Confessions—Special edition

Number-one Singles
1998 "Nice and Slow"

2001 "U Got It Bad"

 "U Remind Me"

2004 "My Boo" (with Alicia Keys)

 "Confessions 2"

 "Burn"

 "Yeah!" (with Lil John and Ludacris)

Selected Television Appearances
1998 *The Bold and the Beautiful*

1999 *Promised Land*; *Moesha*

2000 *Geppetto*; *The Famous Jett Jackson*

2002 *Mad TV*; *Sabrina, the Teenage Witch*; *The Twilight Zone*; *American Dreams*; *7th Heaven*

2003 *Soul Food*; *Punk'd*; *Tinseltown TV*

2004 *T4*; *Live with Regis and Kelly*; *Top of the Pops*; *Last Call with Carson Daly*; *Late Show with David Letterman*; *Saturday Night Live*; *The Tonight Show with Jay Leno*; *Ellen: The Ellen DeGeneres Show*; *Jimmy Kimmel Live*; *On-Air with Ryan Seacrest*; *Good Morning Australia*; *Later with Jools Holland*; *Total Request Live*

2005 *Total Request Live*; *The Oprah Winfrey Show*; *The Tyra Banks Show*; *The Tonight Show with Jay Leno*; *Ellen: The Ellen DeGeneres Show*; *Live with Regis and Kelly*; *Late Night with Conan O'Brien*; *Total Request Live*; *The View*

Film

1998   *The Faculty*

1999   *Light It Up*

         She's All That

2001   *Texas Rangers*

2005   *In the Mix*

Video

1999   *Usher Live*

2001   *MTV 20: Jams*

2002   *Usher: Evolution 8701: Live in Concert*

2004   *VH1 Big in 04*

2005   *Rhythm City Volume One: Caught Up*

Awards

1997   Soul Train Music Awards: Best R&B/Soul Single—Male

1998   Billboard Music Awards: R&B Artist of the Year; Hot 100 Singles Artist of the Year; Billboard Music Awards: R&B Group of the Year; Artist of the Year

2001   Soul Train Music Awards: Best R&B/Soul Album—Male; Grammy Awards: Best Male R&B Vocal Performance; Grammy Awards: Best Male R&B Vocal Performance; Billboard Music Awards: Top R&B/Hip-Hop Artist; Billboard R&B/Hip-Hop Awards: Top R&B/Hip-Hop Artist—Male; Top R&B/Hip-Hop Singles Artist

2004   Soul Train Music Awards: Best RB/Soul Single—Male, Best RB/Soul Album—Male, Best RB/Soul—Group, Band, or Duo (with Alicia Keys), Best RB/Soul or Rap Dance Cut (featuring Ludacris and Lil John), Sammy Davis Jr. Award for Entertainer of the Year; People's Choice Awards: Favorite Male Singer; Favorite Combined Forces (with Ludacris and Lil John); MTV Video Music Awards: Dance Video of the Year (with Ludacris and Lil John), Male Video of the Year (with Ludacris and Lil John); Grammy Awards: Best Rap/Sung Collaboration (with Ludacris and Lil John), Best R&B Vocal Performance, Best R&B Performance—Duo or Group with Vocals (with Alicia Keys), Best Male R&B Vocal Performance; Best Contemporary R&B Album

Books

Chang, Jeff. *Can't Stop, Won't Stop: A History of the Hip-Hop Generation.* New York: St. Martin's Press, 2005.

Kulkarni, Neil. *Hip Hop: Bring the Noise (Stories Behind Every Song).* New York: Thunder's Mouth Press, 2004.

Laslo, Cynthia. *Brandy.* Danbury, Conn.: Children's Press, 2000.

Nelson, George. *Hip-Hop America.* New York: Penguin, 2005.

Talmadge, Morgan. *Usher.* New York: Rosen, 2001.

Magazine Articles

Blatt, Jessica. "Usher: Rock n' Soul: He May Have a Rock-Hard Six-Pack, but It's Usher's Soft Heart That Will Melt You Like Butter." *CosmoGirl!*, June 1, 2005.

"The Remix of Usher: Red-Hot R&B Superstar Still Sizzling 'Yeah!' Yeah!! Yeah!!!" *Jet*, February 7, 2005.

Smith, Danyel. "Hot for Usher: Jeans King, Louis Prince, Sex Walker: The Soul Singer Talks About His Love Affair with the 1980s and the Mysteries of Sex, Swagger and Shape." *W*, October 1, 2004.

Winters, Rebecca. "Usher Plays Dress-Up." *Time*, February 14, 2005.

Zaslow, Jeffrey. "Straight Talk: Usher." *USA Weekend*, August 7–9, 1998.

Web Sites

Arista Records: Usher
www.aristarec.com

GETMUSIC
www.getmusic.com

New Look Foundation
www.ushersnewlook.org

Rock on the Net: Usher
www.rockonthenet.com/artists-u/usher_main.htm

Usher World
www.usherworld.com

autobiographical—told or written by a writer about him- or herself.

ballad—a slow, romantic popular song.

charisma—the ability to inspire enthusiasm, interest, or affection in others by means of personal charm.

choreographer—the person who plans dances to accompany music.

collaboration—two or more people working together on the same project.

debut—doing something for the first time.

decoys—replicas used to divert attention.

evacuees—people removed from a dangerous situation and moved to a safer location.

executives—senior managers in a company.

funk—popular music style derived from jazz, blues, and soul, and characterized by a heavy rhythmic bass and backbeat.

gold—the sale of 500,000 albums.

Gospel—a distinctively American religious music that is associated with Christianity and is based on the melodies of folk music blended with elements of African American spirituals and jazz.

jam—improvised music.

mayhem—absolute chaos or severe disruption.

mentors—older, more experienced people who help younger, less experienced people.

opened—performed before the main attraction.

perfectionist—someone who demands perfection in all things.

platinum—album sales of more than 2 million.

producer—someone who organizes and supervises the making of an album.

R&B—rhythm and blues; a mixing of blues and jazz.

simultaneously—done at the same time.

subculture—a smaller group within a larger group with ideas and behaviors that differ from the larger group.

tracks—separate pieces of music or song on a disk, tape, or record.

tribute—something done to show gratitude, praise, or admiration.

Raymond Lord got a bachelor's degree in writing and literature at Houghton College in New York State. He went on and got his master's degree from Geneseo State College. Mr. Lord wrote for his college newspaper and was coeditor for the college literary magazine. His work has appeared in a variety of publications.

Picture Credits

page

2: PRNewsFoto/NMI
8: UPI Photo/Roger Williams
11: Dimitri Halkidis/WENN
13: Zuma Press/Nancy Kaszerman
14: Zuma Press/Wile E.
16: Zuma Press/Steven Tackeff
19: Shannon McCollum/WENN
20: Zuma Press/Steve Tackeff
22: UPI/Bill Greenblatt
25: Everrett Collection
26: Miramax Films/NMI
28: Zuma Press/Nancy Kaszerman
31: Zuma Press/URH/UPPA

32: Zuma Press/Rahav Segev
34: PRNewsFoto/NMI
37: Brian Prahl/ Splash News
38: KRT/NMI
41: KRT/Tim Grant
43: PRNewsFoto/NMI
44: INFGoff
46: Lions Gate Films/NMI
48: Ace Pictures/Kristin Callahan
51: KRT/Phil Masturzo
53: AFP/Anna Zieminski
54: PRNewsFoto/NMI

Front cover: Tsuni/Gamma
Back cover: Zuma Press/UPPA